The Metaverse

Gain Insight Into The Exciting Future

of the Internet

Vicky V. Choudhary

Foreword

The Metaverse internet fad has recently overtaken the internet. The metaverse is an old concept that's had recently gained broad recognition. The metaverse represents a different way of making use of the internet. It has the potential to revolutionize how users use the internet forever. They let users to engage with material in novel ways and have the potential to shape the future of the internet. It is a digital cosmos comprised of several interrelated areas. Those who believe in the metaverse believe that it may be utilized to boost productivity. This book is all about exploring the ways in which the internet has evolved over the years and the ways in which it will continue to evolve. This book shares insights on why we should all be excited for these new concepts of virtual world. This book helps you understand the world of Metaverse. It explains the Metaverse Ecosystem and its architecture. The book further discusses various aspects associated with the Metaverse Ecosystem.

Enjoy your reading.

Have a good time ahead.

Table of Contents

Chapter 1
Introduction to Metaverse

The idea of the Metaverse has existed for quite some time. It refers to the idea of a communal virtual reality setting where people may communicate and share information. Although the idea has received attention from several developers, it hasn't yet become widely used in commercial activity. According to some, the Metaverse has the potential to significantly disrupt the technology industry. Others, though, are cautious due to its potential.

Defining Metaverse

A metaverse is a made-up virtual world with several interconnected virtual realities. A network of links can bind these universes together. Users may access and engage with content from any of them thanks to this. It's common to think of metaverses as the next step in the development of online social networking. They provide a more immersive experience than products that are already available. As a result, users may communicate with one another within the self-contained realm known as the Metaverse. The Metaverse will benefit from three important factors. It will first and foremost provide a more dynamic and engaging experience than the current Internet. Second, users will have the option to create their virtual reality world. The Metaverse will also act as a platform for social networking and communication. The ability of the metaverse to provide a more immersive experience than the current Internet is perhaps its most salient advantage.

How is the metaverse different from the internet?

The internet is a vast and ever-expanding global network that connects people from all over the world. In contrast, the metaverse is a virtual reality environment in which users may interact and converse in a more immersive and realistic manner.

Chapter 2
Evolution of the Internet

Before we could understand the world of the metaverse, we must understand the background of the internet. Exploring the evolution of the internet will immensely help us in availing a clear picture of what the metaverse is. Let's begin with it.

The internet and the web are not interchangeable terms. Both are distinct yet connected entities. The Internet is a network of networks. Millions of computers are internationally linked to form a network in which any computer may communicate with any other computer. The World Wide Web is a method of gaining access to information over the internet. It accomplishes this by showing web pages on a browser. Hyperlinks connect information. It may comprise text, images, audio, or video [1].

Web1.0 refers to the initial generation of the internet. It is sometimes referred to as an informational web. It evolved from 1991 onwards, following its creation by Tim Berners Lee in 1989-1991. In this environment, users can simply read and distribute content on websites. Web 1.0 was primarily a source of information generated by a small group of authors for a huge group of mostly uninformed consumers. It was primarily static pages with little potential for true participation. Web2.0 is a platform that allows us to create, distribute, and alter the content. The term "Web 2.0" originally appeared in 1999. The Internet shifted toward a system in which the user was actively engaged. The phrase "Web 2.0" gained popularity during the inaugural O'Reilly Media Web 2.0 conference in 2004 [1].

Web 3.0 is the internet's third generation, in which websites and apps will be able to process information in a sophisticated human-like manner. This may be accomplished via technologies such as machine learning (ML), Big Data, decentralized ledger technology (DLT), and so on. Tim Berners-Lee, the creator of the World Wide Web, dubbed Web 3.0 the Semantic Web. Its goal was to create a more independent, intelligent, and open internet. As web3.0 evolves, big IT platforms are looking at augmented reality as the next computing platform change. There are efforts made to integrate aspects of the physical and digital worlds. Virtual reality, augmented reality, gaming, and immersive online communities may all be used to achieve this. All of them are fostering the development of a Web 3.0 that is more decentralized. As a result, a new technological period known as the metaverse is created by the fusing of many technologies, including software, hardware devices, AR/VR/MR, as well as specific sound and geographic capabilities [1].

Understanding Web 1.0

Web 1.0 is the term used to describe the first version of the web. This is the "read-only web," in Berners-words. Lee's Web 1.0 was designed as a platform for businesses to share information. It merely lets users view and searches for content on websites. Here, users are unable to interact with the page's content (no comments, no responses, no quotes, etc) [1].

The Good Points About Web 1.0

There is just single access. This implies that the only person who may alter the content is the author. As a result, the contents are not altered without the creator's consent. The benefits of web 1.0 include student autonomy, exposure to many literacies, and genuine resources and experiences. It permits a minimal amount of interaction [1].

The Bad Points About Web 1.0

High levels of engagement are necessary for online applications, especially dynamic web applications. We could need automatically refreshed database material. Users will be able to quickly access updated material thanks to this. Web 1.0 failed in this area because this kind of interaction is essential for apps. Only clicks and page refreshes are permitted. With Web 1.0, rich user experiences will not be feasible. Every time we want to check the material, we will need to refresh it. Additionally, WAP browsing—the loading of Web 1.0 applications—was not possible in mobile browsers. Another problem with Web 1.0 technology is this. [1].

The Worst Downsides of Web 1.0

The vast majority of users on Web 1.0 were consumers of content. The designers require access to a server to build their website. Strong programming abilities are required. To create content, they must write lengthy, intricate code. Additionally, users cannot change the material in web1.0, and viewers are unable to interact with it. Internet traffic and advertising have decreased as a result. Advertisers are searching for fresh approaches to interact with their target markets through conventional media. To be more precise, Web 1.0 is a basic information portal where users are just given access to material and are not given the chance to post, evaluate, or give comments. The website is largely locked and not particularly user-friendly [1].

Understanding Web 2.0

There are a few factors to think about while defining web 2.0. The phrase describes online tools that let users exchange information, work together, and express themselves freely. In contrast to web1.0, web2.0 enables users to create, edit, and update material online. Additionally, it promotes cooperation and aids in the development of collective intelligence [1].

The Good Points About Web 2.0

By enabling simple choice navigation, Web 2.0 fosters excellent user engagement. Examples of Web 2.0 technologies include social networks, blogs, and forums. These might be utilized to accomplish this easy and efficient method of spreading the word. With the use of Web 2.0 technology, a teacher may shift from being an information provider to a facilitator of learning. It can generate more dynamic and interactive learning environments where students may develop, modify, and assess information [1].

Collaboration between students, professors, and subject-matter specialists is made easier by Web 2.0. Additionally, it brings together experts from many professions and a wide range of other people with similar interests. A paradigm shift from instructors and teaching to students and learning has happened with the advent of Web 2.0 technology. Learning that is "student-centered" is the outcome of this. Electronic media advertising may be pricey. However, we can reach a lot of people with less money if we use Online 2.0 technologies like web blogs and social networks. As a result of utilizing Web 2.0 technology, businesses have benefited in several operational areas. Due to better idea-sharing capabilities and expanded access to information specialists, business is now easier to perform. The cheaper cost of operations, travel, and communication technology is another consideration. [1].

Additionally, the time required for marketing has decreased thanks to Web 2.0 technologies. The breadth of the marketing industry has grown. Businesses may more readily spread product information thanks to it. Perhaps more crucially, it makes it possible to solicit client input and even include them in the creation of new products. Web 2.0 has led to an increase in e-commerce or online business. This led several businesses to start-up e-commerce businesses. These businesses employ services like cloud product marketing, digital marketing, SEO specialists, payment gateways, and internet banking. These are all currently included in supply chain transactions. Additionally, there is a noticeable improvement in customer relationship management and a higher level of employee satisfaction. This was made possible by the businesses' capacity to develop closer relationships with their clients. As a consequence, brand recall and awareness have grown. Relations with partners and suppliers have also improved in similar ways. Additionally, the medical and health industry is gradually starting to use Web 2.0 strategies and technology. Social networking, blogging, and exchanging health information are a few of these activities. Health 2.0 serves as the umbrella term for this new trend. It will have a big impact on how medicine is practiced in the future [1].

Web-users using conventional e-Health technology can only take information passively. However, Health 2.0 gives web users the power to actively alter online content. Additionally, Web 2.0 has the potential to dramatically advance e-health in rural areas. Along with several medical websites and portals providing various medical and health services [1]. These are discussed as follows.

• People can share their experiences and knowledge about various ailments through online support groups and virtual communities. Along with that, it aids in fostering mutual emotional support [1].

• The Open Source, Web-based Electronic Health Records (EHR) system is another service. It includes an online learning component powered by Web 2.0 to enhance continuous medical education and raise public awareness [1].

• Doctors may electronically consult with and treat patients thanks to telehealth/telemedicine. Through virtual doctor visits, patients can consult a physician online and receive essential medications in addition to medical advice [1].

Web2.0 is quickly becoming a useful resource for international visitors. They can get travel advice and suggestions for tourist suppliers. The notion of "Tourism 2.0" emerged alongside the web2.0 movement. It described a fresh and modern manner of experiencing tourism. Web 2.0 technologies, such as social networks and podcasts, have made it possible for many individuals to acquire information and connect with tourist service providers at any time. This is feasible without incurring significant expenditures, and it may be accomplished in a variety of ways. This includes anything from writing in chat rooms to audio-visual aspects about tourism demand and supply. Aside from the aforementioned areas, web2.0 has made major contributions to a variety of industries. Agriculture, online education, financial services, and other industries are examples of this [1].

The Bad Points About Web 2.0

Web 2.0 is vulnerable to vandalism since many users have the power to own and manage data on the site. A person can purposefully disrupt or destroy the website's contents, including impersonating other websites. This can result in skewed information, raising concerns about the reliability of the information provided on the sites. Web2.0 apps are publicly available and dynamically built nowadays. This aspect of web2.0 adds to its appeal. However, it raises the danger of security breaches. Many website owners prefer that developers focus on usefulness rather than security. As a result, developers may fail to take measures such as verifying user input on websites regularly. These pages are appealing to hackers as a result of more standard attack routes such as e-mail attachments [1].

Web 2.0 has been used by hackers to spread worms that perform dangerous actions outside of the browser. The consumers are oblivious of what they are doing as a result. Additionally, they publish harmful stuff on social media that seems real. Consider the case below. Content that contains code or malware that may be used to carry out destructive actions may be uploaded by a User/Hacker. Sometimes, hackers will provide software that purports to remove viruses. nonetheless, inserts a Trojan virus onto social networking websites. People these days are far too dependent on social networking platforms. Users are clicking every link without thinking. And many programmers and hackers profit from this. Malicious programs, including key loggers, may be uploaded by hackers. This could capture keystrokes made by victims, including credit cards [1].

The Worst Downsides of Web 2.0

Web 2.0 is making a sensation because it pushes the capabilities of websites. But according to experts, security has taken a backseat in the hurry to add features. Web 2.0 worms can therefore propagate when a user visits an infected website without being visible in an open window. Social platform assaults often work by obtaining users' login information when they log in, giving hackers access to their accounts. This data is then utilized to covertly gather personal information from users' internet friends and coworkers. [1].

In recent years, geo-tagged images have grown in popularity. When posting photos to social media, people tag them with their locations. Some programs offer a Geo-tagging function that, unless the user actively turns it off, automatically marks the user's current location in a snapshot. This may disclose private information, such as one's residence and travel patterns. The threat to one's regular way of life is caused by this. Additionally, those who use social media more frequently are more inclined to like their friends' postings. By abusing this trust, cybercriminals. Some of the most frequent social media assaults include hacking techniques like Likejacking, Clickjacking, etc. User data and login passwords are being stolen increasingly frequently as internet tools and applications progress [1].

One of Web 2.0's and Web 1.0's biggest drawbacks is the client-server architecture. This centralized system was in charge of the users' life in many different ways and held all the data. The risk to people's privacy from this situation is therefore quite high. A decentralized network, however, is not susceptible to the risk of data breaches. Your private information is not in anyone's control. No centralized server will exist. Throughout the whole network, the data will be scattered. Blockchain is elevating this infrastructure to a completely new level as a result of the cryptocurrency revolution. From our conventional centralized system, we can now go to decentralizing data structures. Individuals' private information won't be traded like a commodity as a consequence [1].

Web 3.0- A decentralized web

Web 2.0 and previous versions relied on centralized servers. Web 3.0, on the other hand, features a decentralized network that is more user-centric. Web3.0 takes the form of new technologies. Cryptocurrencies, virtual and augmented reality, artificial intelligence, and other technology are examples of this. A transformation in our understanding of the internet is driving the Web3.0 movement. This affects how we, as a society, perceive and value the Internet, which is being supported by new technology [1].

The objective of Web3.0 is to establish an Internet that is owned and operated by the people. Web3.0 is concerned with reengineering current internet services and goods to benefit consumers. It is similar to an open internet since it is based on open protocols and transparent blockchain networks. It is available to all users. Consumers might interface with these protocols via blended apps that give convenient methods to connect with the underlying technology. Facilitating safe data transfers, automatic cryptocurrency payments, and easy ownership transfers will profoundly transform the way humans and machines interact [1].

Web 3.0 does not have a standardized definition. However, it does contain some unique features. These characteristics are discussed as follows.

• _Semantic Web:_ Web 3.0 is referred to as the Semantic Web. It is the next step in the evolution of the internet. By utilizing the powers of artificial intelligence, it is possible to analyze data with intelligence comparable to that of a human (AI). As a result, a machine can process knowledge rather than simply words. This is done by the application of techniques similar to human logical thinking and inference. This has resulted in more meaningful consequences. They can identify user interests. As a consequence, they can help customers discover what they want faster and understand how goods are connected [1].

• _Ubiquitous:_ We'll be able to access the Internet from anywhere at any time thanks to Web 3.0. In the future, web-connected gadgets won't just be restricted to PCs and smartphones, as they were in web 2.0. The Internet of Things will use technology to enable the creation of several new types of intelligent devices (IoT) [1].

• _Decentralized nature:_ Web 3.0 will provide more flexibility to both authors and consumers in general. Web 3.0 will ensure that consumers always retain control over their online data by employing decentralized networks. Because of its decentralized structure, the future generation of the internet is also predicted to be more dependable. As a result, the possibility of a single point of failure is eliminated [1].

• _Trustless governance system:_ We may circumvent the restrictions of our old governance system by using Web3.0. To ensure the supply of products and services, our existing governance structure employs legal contracts. Enforcing these contracts, on the other hand, is a time-consuming and expensive procedure that includes middlemen at every stage. As a result, while a formal agreement protects you, the system is inefficient, prone to errors, and prone to delays. This challenge can be addressed by developing a trustless governance system based on smart contracts in Web 3.0. In other words, users may connect on the network both openly and privately without having to go through an intermediary, which might put them in danger. Smart contracts are bits of open-source code that include criteria that both parties agree on before they begin. When the preset circumstances are satisfied, the contract is automatically executed. Smart contracts enable services to be verified and readily enforced.

Services may be obtained from anywhere in the world. Contract monitoring and transaction auditing would be significantly reduced as a result [1].

• *Blockchain technology:* Web3.0 provides unparalleled levels of user data protection and privacy. Data scattered over numerous systems might pose privacy problems. This issue is addressed by blockchain in Web 3.0. Because there is no single point of failure, this is the case. The data ledger is replicated on each node in the network. As a result, a breach would need hackers to have concurrent access to a large number of nodes. It is incredibly tough and expensive to breach that degree of protection [1].

• *Digital identities:* Web 3.0 introduces secure digital identities. These also contribute to data privacy protection. Digital identities will be encrypted, anonymous, and platform-independent. These digital identities will be linked with user permission. This implies that, unlike Web 2.0, users may be asked whether or not they want to see adverts [1].

• *Tokenization:* Furthermore, the digitalization of assets via tokenization is the key to Web 3.0 innovation. The process of transforming assets and rights into a digital representation, or token, is known as tokenization. This token is usable on the blockchain network. Cryptocurrency and fungible tokens are digital currencies that can be readily transferred across networks, enabling a new business model that democratizes money and commerce. Non-fungible tokens (NFTs) are data units that represent one-of-a-kind assets like avatars, digital art, or trading cards. Users can own and commercialize these assets for their benefit [1].

The Bad Points About Web 3.0

The concept of web 3.0 offers several prospects for growth and development. However, it poses security problems. Web3.0 has given rise to a new breed of cyberthreat. While decentralized data and services limit the number of single points of failure. They do, however, raise the danger of data being exposed to a broader spectrum of risks. These include both traditional threats and strategies specific to blockchain networks and interfaces [1].

• *Lack of oversight:* Experts fear that decentralization will exacerbate the difficulties associated with monitoring and regulating Web 3.0. This might result in a rise in cybercrime, online abuse, and other issues [1].

• *Smart contract hacks:* The logic contained in blockchain services is the target of smart contract logic attacks. Malware is created by attackers. This is then deployed as malicious smart contract code on the blockchain. All of the typical smart contract features are included in malicious smart contracts. However, they behave weirdly. These attacks have targeted interoperability, crypto-loan services, project governance, and wallet functionality. Smart contract logic hacks present major legal concerns as well. This is because smart contracts are sometimes not legally protected or are dispersed among states [1].

• _Seed phrase attack:_ The great majority of security problems involving Web 3.0 users are the result of social engineering tactics such as wallet cloning. Customer support employees are impersonated by hackers. As a result, they offer to answer publicly posted Twitter or Discord server requests from users. Criminals will monitor these platforms and contact people to provide "help." They ultimately persuade them to reveal their seed phrases. Anyone who has access to the seed phrase (private key) of a bitcoin wallet can clone it and use it as their own [1].

• _Partial decentralization of dApps:_ The Ethereum network is responsible for the cryptocurrency ether (ETH). It allows you to access thousands of decentralized applications (dApps). It is now the largest decentralized network controlled by a community. Decentralized Applications (dApps) are not commonly distributed. Instead of a centralized database, they are just responsive web pages with states and permissions kept on the blockchain. Many blockchain solutions include user-controlled cryptographic key management. The user has a private key that they use for their wallet, application, and authentication server. It is catastrophic to lose or lose hold of this key. Many individuals utilize web2.0 platforms to maintain users' private keys and wallets as custodians or mediators. As a result, we are not entirely prepared to operate with a decentralized web. However, one consideration for web 3.0 security professionals will be the administration of multiple cryptographic keys without relying on centralized institutions [1].

• *Information quality:* In Web 1.0, the reputation of publications was used to determine accuracy. Web 2.0 has degraded data quality. This increased the effectiveness of misinformation and deception on the internet. As a result, accuracy checks must be incorporated into the agreement to accept machine-managed data in web 3.0 [1].

The Worst Downsides of Web 3.0

In the web3.0 world, there are several forms of assaults. Because the technology is still in its early stages, new sorts of assaults may arise. Some attacks resemble typical credential attacks seen on web2.0. However, some are exclusive to web3.0 [1]. Various types of security risks are associated with web3.0. are discussed as follows.

• _Wormhole Bridge:_ Blockchains have already had several serious security breaches in their very short existence as underpinning technology. The Wormhole Bridge is a mechanism for blockchain interoperability. Users and decentralized apps can utilize it to move assets across blockchains. This causes tremendous alarm among web experts [1].

• _Data manipulation:_ Intentional modification of data that will be used to train AI is a big cybersecurity threat. People can invent false data to achieve the desired results. This has the potential to make AI the world's largest misinformation system. This provides a significant problem for cybersecurity specialists in identifying, blocking and removing deceptive data [1].

• _Data confidentiality:_ Constant data breaches jeopardize private information. Furthermore, content may be mistakenly published or stored in an unsecured area. When computers scan data and store it in their knowledge base, the likelihood of private information being discovered and utilized rises substantially. It is necessary to develop a defensive mechanism to prevent the distribution of secret information. To do this, cybersecurity executives must increase their defenses [1].

• _Enhanced spam:_ A massive library of integrated and interconnected information will exist in a Web 3.0 environment. This will open up more risky routes for spam assaults to spread. Adversaries can propagate spam by targeting, exploiting, and polluting certain resources. This is possible with websites, search engines, and programs that use the entire internet as a database. By injecting harmful JavaScript code or ransomware into an application, these spam operations might send it to every user [1].

• _Crypto-jacking:_ The hazards of crypto-jacking will rise as web3.0 evolves. Cybercrime includes crypto-jacking. It entails cybercriminals mining bitcoin on people's devices without their knowledge. Cybercriminals compromise devices to install crypto-jacking software. The program is running in the background. It enables bitcoin mining and theft from cryptocurrency wallets. Hackers can silently mine cryptocurrency on a victim's device using one of two ways. To begin, persuade the victim to click on a malicious link in an email. They install crypto mining software on their PC in this manner. The second method is to infect a website or an online advertisement with JavaScript code. This runs automatically when the victim's browser is launched [1].

• _Rug Pull:_ Rug pulls are a lucrative fraud in which a cryptocurrency creator promotes a new project. It frequently promotes a new coin to investors and then disappears with a large sum of money [1].

• _Ice phishing:_ The "ice phishing" method does not entail stealing private keys. Rather, it includes duping a user into signing a transaction that grants the attacker approval over the user's tokens. The attackers can collect approvals over time by employing an ice phishing assault. They can then rapidly empty the victim's wallets [1].

Chapter 3
Let's Explore the Metaverse

The concept of a metaverse is not novel. In his 1992 cyberpunk novel Snow Crash, science fiction novelist Neal Stephenson invented the term "metaverse" [9]. He demonstrated a 3D virtual environment with individuals depicted as avatars. They might engage with each other as well as with artificially intelligent beings. It combines technology aspects such as virtual reality, augmented reality, and video. As a result, the users "live" in a digital realm. The metaverse is presently being theorized in many sections and portions. However, a comprehensive metaverse is considered the next computing platform and internet extension [1].

The video game Second Life has effectively incorporated the initial metaverse concept. A video game and website called Second Life was introduced in 2003. It enables people to sign up and participate in a second virtual existence. In the virtual world, they may adopt any identity and perform any part. Web3D enables users to interact with virtual worlds as an avatar. They can therefore go exploring, interact with other residents, engage in both individual and/or group activities, and so on. They would do this in the real world as well. The idea of a metaverse has long been exploited in movies. Examples of movies with a metaverse theme include Gamer, Ready Player One, The Matrix, Minority Report, Terminator, and Surrogates. In each of these movies, a real person uses a tool or instrument to assume a part in a virtual setting. The most recent film of this kind is Free Guy (2021). It is an illustration of a metaverse in which a video game's AI character serves as the primary character. And this character develops feelings for an actual player. Although the concept of the metaverse is not new. There wasn't the technology to make it happen. A lot quicker internet, more data storage, and more powerful computation are all required for 3D things. Furthermore, they need AR, VR, and XR (Extended Reality) equipment to display 3D things in real-time [1].

What is Extended Reality?

Extended Reality (XR) is the fusion of interactive computer visuals and human interaction. Both the actual world and the virtual world share this. Extended Reality is, in essence, a superset of Augmented Reality (AR), Virtual Reality (VR), and Mixed Reality (MR) [2].

The notion of Extended Reality (XR) emerged as a result of technologies such as Augmented and Virtual reality. These technologies were employed by developers and IT businesses all across the world. The notion of Extended Reality has been featured in several science fiction films (XR). However, running it in the actual world is considerably different from controlling it on the screen. The following section discusses the technical aspects of Extended Reality (XR). Let's look at the technologies that are utilized to generate Extended Reality (XR) [2].

1. *Augmented Reality (AR):* Imaginations and virtual things are projected into the actual environment according to the theory of augmented reality. No virtual or computer-generated images are present while using augmented reality. In contrast, it just gives digital devices the illusion of an illusion. Access to the outside world is still available to users. In all realms, they can completely converse. The most prevalent instance of augmented reality is the game Pokémon GO. With the aid of digital devices, individuals may therefore engage with both the actual world and a virtual one. The filters that we see in several apps are another kind of augmented reality. These just provide the appearance that they are present but are not [2].

2. *Virtual Reality (VR):* Users in virtual reality are immersed in a completely virtual environment. They can only interact in the virtual world. The pictures produced are primarily computer-generated, with fake things made to appear real. Every aspect of virtual reality is felt by the users. To immerse consumers in this world, special VR gear is required. These gadgets provide individuals with a 360-degree perspective of the virtual environment. These gadgets are intended to provide consumers with a more realistic illusion [2].

3. *Mixed Reality (MR):* Mixed reality combines both augmented and virtual reality. This allows for simultaneous interaction with the actual world and the digital one. Utilizing specialized MR gear, users can see their environment. These MR technologies are both more expensive and powerful than VR ones. However, these gadgets enable you to digitally engage with your environment. For instance, putting on an MR gadget will let you see everything around you. You can close the windows, throw a ball, or do whatever else you choose. Your MR headset will display all of this digitally. However, things will continue to be as they are in reality. Numerous businesses are spending a significant amount of money to do in-depth studies in this area of reality [2].

Simply said, Extended Reality (XR) enables people to travel virtually. They may communicate with others on XR and experience the same sensation as if they were physically present there. Thus, it combines all three technologies—AR, VR, and MR [2].

Chapter 4
The Metaverse Ecosystem

Let us understand the metaverse ecosystem. The following chapter discusses the architecture of the metaverse.

Infrastructure

In the context of the metaverse, infrastructure generally refers to the technological infrastructure that supports the metaverse. Wi-Fi, cloud computing and 5G are among the networking technologies included in the architecture. All of this is in addition to the use of high-tech materials like GPUs [3].

One of the key features of the metaverse is that it will continue to grow. As a result, the metaverse infrastructure must ensure ultra-low latency, insanely fast speeds, and increased capacity. A solid infrastructure serves as the foundation for smooth, value-based experiences for all metaverse users [3].

With recent attempts by various tech businesses, the emphasis on infrastructure as a crucial entrance among metaverse elements becomes obvious. The industrial alliance provides critical opportunities for enhancing the metaverse infrastructure to encourage the growth of the metaverse ecosystem [3].

Human Interface Technologies

As previously stated, infrastructure is a critical component of the metaverse. As a result, one would naturally turn to human interface technology. Users can enter the metaverse by using technologies such as VR headsets, haptics, AR glasses, and many more [3].

Human interface technologies aid in transferring people into the metaverse's endless immersive places. Human interface technologies for the metaverse, on the other hand, are being improved. Smartphones, laptops, tablets, and PCs may all be used to connect to the metaverse. These gadgets must be enhanced with the appropriate functionalities [3].

Digital Avatars

Digital avatars are another major highlight among the important components of the metaverse. Digital avatars are a key component in the creation of the metaverse. Users can develop digital avatars to convey their thoughts and sentiments innovatively in the metaverse. You may utilize the metaverse features to create personalized digital avatars. As a result, you may take a digital duplicate of your favorite superhero with you [3].

Interestingly, the ability to create and customize digital avatars in the metaverse brings up new opportunities for gamification. As a result, digital avatars enhance the foundation for an engaging and immersive metaverse experience [3].

Decentralized System

Decentralization would be the next big component. The metaverse is envisioned as an open, shared reality. Users can travel effortlessly among platforms in this universe. Users of the Metaverse might develop their own virtual experiences and assets with monetary worth. They can exchange them without the need for centralized authorities. Decentralization is a prominent element of the metaverse at this point [3].

Some of the most important technologies enabling metaverse democratization include blockchain, edge computing, and artificial intelligence. Users may obtain total control and ownership of their assets and experiences in the metaverse with the aid of decentralization. As a result, the decentralization of the metaverse is critical in deciding user freedom. As a result, the decentralization characteristic immediately distinguishes the metaverse from the internet as we know it now [3].

3D World

For obvious reasons, spatial computing is the next critical component in the metaverse architecture. There can be no 3D worlds without spatial computing capabilities. As a result, 3D visualization tools and modeling frameworks are also critical components for the metaverse's growth [3].

Security

There's no reason why you shouldn't use security features in the metaverse. Cyber security has been a significant concern for many businesses throughout the world. As a result, security problems pose negative difficulties for the metaverse. To address such problems, the metaverse provides security elements such as ethical and privacy norms throughout the ecosystem [3].

The importance of security as one of the fundamental components of the metaverse cannot be emphasized, even if the metaverse is still in its infancy. Improved user identity and protection rules are required for the metaverse. It is reasonable to highlight the necessity for ethical behavior given that many businesses are working on the creation of the metaverse [3].

Creator Economy

The creator economy is valued more highly than all the other components of the metaverse. How will the users of the metaverse benefit from it? Well, playing games and such things are undoubtedly entertaining. That, however, does not provide a compelling argument for investing in pricey technology to participate in the metaverse [3].

You may still join Zoom meetings on your phone and use your laptops and PCs to participate in online workplaces. Users of the metaverse can access design tools through the creator economy to produce digital goods and experiences. These assets are theirs to possess and trade on online markets. Consequently, one of the major aspects of the metaverse that highlights its usefulness in the future is the creator economy [3].

Discovery

It is anticipated that the metaverse would develop into a sizable 3D environment with a variety of virtual locations.

Therefore, it makes perfect sense to add the necessary elements to aid in the exploration of the various virtual places. The metaverse's architecture's discovery component may lay a solid groundwork for increasing its level of interaction [3].

The content engine is one of the key components of metaverse architecture that may aid in discovery. The integration of several elements, including social media, reviews, advertisements, and ratings, by the content engine, can increase engagement [3].

Experience

The metaverse's last design element is perhaps the most crucial one in determining how the metaverse functions. You can discover how the metaverse promises immersive experiences if you go more and comprehend it [3].

Anyone would find it nearly impossible to use a virtual environment without something to do there. Experiences are therefore necessary for the formation of the metaverse. You may think of them as the virtual reality versions of digital applications for events, work, shopping, and gaming [3].

Practically speaking, the metaverse is an unpopulated, empty virtual space without any experiences. The encounters aid in converting several actual experiences into a virtual setting. The promise of the metaverse, which is the most significant of all, is to unite all analog and digital experiences [3].

Consider the case below. Remote collaboration between students and professionals is possible in shared learning and working areas. The potential for more engaging user experiences in the metaverse is presented by the combination of the various scattered experiences under a single setting. Teachers might conduct field trips for their pupils without actually going to the destination. Additionally, the metaverse experiences could offer more opportunities for hands-on, practical learning [3].

The architecture of the metaverse is thoroughly explained, showing how it can develop in the future. However, many of you might think that everything here will only ever exist as a concept on paper. However, as you look at the numerous metaverse instances now in use, you will quickly dispel such notions [3].

The overall perception of the metaverse's elements leads one to believe that it was designed as a ground-breaking technical innovation. Science fiction and movies have created vivid images of the metaverse and what it should be like. However, the attributes of the metaverse aid in making the metaverse's vision a reality. It is easy to see how the metaverse's constituents establish its fundamental capabilities. The metaverse would have a wide range of additional elements as it expands.

Chapter 5
Characteristics of the Metaverse

The distinctive characteristics of an immersive metaverse can offer essential assistance for generating the one-of-a-kind experience that everyone seeks. This chapter discusses the key qualities of the metaverse.

Persistence

Persistence is a key aspect of the metaverse that deserves special attention. One of the prevalent ideas about the metaverse is that it is a virtual reality environment. To enter the virtual world of the metaverse, you must put on your VR headsets [3].

But what happens if you take the headset off? Does that represent the end of the metaverse's world? No. In actuality, the metaverse keeps functioning even if your power is off. Imagine yourself participating in an online multiplayer game where other players go on even if you are not there [3].

Experiences in virtual reality are only available from the individual business or brand that is providing them. The metaverse, on the other hand, is an endless, active reality. It's just like the actual world here. As a result, perseverance stands out as one of the metaverse's most notable features. It makes it always accessible [3].

Realism

Realism is the primary quality needed for creating various metaverse kinds. Only when an encounter feels realistic do you feel involved. The user experience in 3D worlds is based on how emotionally engaged the users are with the surroundings. Your 3D digital avatars should be exact replicas of your real-world behavior [4].

Sight

The need for sight is emphasized in the following key feature required for various metaverse scenarios. How can you interact with an environment you can't see? Virtual world advancement has minimized indirectness while increasing knowledge on par with the actual world. Virtual worlds have gone a long way in terms of appearance, thanks to the skillful use of real-time computer graphics, graphics technology, and algorithms [4].

Flat polygons are no longer used in graphics rendering. Smooth shading, customizable shaders, and texture mapping are the foundations of virtual environments. Modern 3D and virtual reality experiences will be powered by the ongoing advancement of display technology, graphics algorithms, and computing power [4].

Touch

In the metaverse, we're all talking about immersive experiences with sight, sound, and reality. At the same time, it is critical to call attention to touch. Physical sensations are required for users to engage with things in virtual worlds. Haptics, which simply translates virtual interactions into physical contact, is one of the most prevalent technologies that provide touch functions in virtual environments [4].

Sound

Verbal communication is another critical feature that cannot be overlooked when it comes to vital metaverse design qualities. To build interactions in the virtual world, you would need to talk and listen much as in the actual world. Verbal communication is a necessary characteristic that facilitates consumers' immediate involvement with virtual environments [4].

In reality, speaking and listening in virtual environments such as the metaverse encourages user participation. This is superior to interpreting virtual postures, gestures, and faces [4].

As a result, the ambient sound will be an essential component of any future metaverse use cases. The experience of sound in virtual environments can change thanks to three-dimensional spatial sound and other technologies like binaural rendering [4].

Ubiquity

Everyone must have unrestricted access to the metaverse. It ought to be reachable from any place. Additionally, the growth of wearable technology offers sufficient justification for the same [4].

In addition, the metaverse offers users in the virtual world unique identities. Your virtual presence, the material you create and share, and the assets you possess and trade all make up your identity in the virtual world. Users may readily access diverse material in the metaverse areas using a variety of virtual identities [4].

Gestures and Expressions

The metaverse design elements also heavily factor in non-verbal communication. You require facial and body language in the metaverse that accurately reflects users' true feelings [4].

AI, machine learning, and VR technologies are all transforming the play-to-earn gestures and emotions genre of virtual world games. Expressions may now be translated, processed, and recorded more easily [4].

Interoperability

There are several levels when you examine the internet as it now exists. You have several networks and subnetworks that encourage user participation. In the real world, when someone relocates to a new area, their identity follows them. In the actual world, people may move their assets around without noticeably changing them [4].

Interoperability in the metaverse design should assist to make this possible as well. Interoperability will enable smooth transitions between various metaverse virtual worlds. Numerous real-world operations, procedures, and systems will be compelled to move to the metaverse. The metaverse may become the seamless virtual world that everyone wants with the correct standards and well-defined levels of interoperability [4].

Bottom line

The core characteristics present promising prospects for the future development of various metaverse kinds. It's crucial to consider how the metaverse could be able to accomplish all of these qualities, though.

Chapter 6
Timeline of Significant Events

We have so far learned about the development of the internet, the fundamental ideas behind the metaverse, and its ecosystem. Let's look at the subsequent occurrences throughout the metaverse conceptual evolution given that we have a foundational understanding of other related technologies. This timeline paints a clear picture of how the development of various technologies assisted professionals, either directly or indirectly, in the construction of the metaverse's framework.

The advent of the Internet (1991)

Tim Berners-Lee published the first official request for collaboration on the World Wide Web sometime in 1991. The internet had only begun to take off at this point [5].

Snow Crash (1992)

The word "metaverse" was invented the following year by science fiction writer Neal Stephenson in his 1992 novel Snow Crash. As previously stated, people communicate with one other and software agents in this story as avatars. They did it in a three-dimensional virtual universe based on a real-world metaphor [5].

Proof of Work (1993)

This word and idea were first used in the realm of computer security to combat email spamming. Later, proof work became one of the key methods for confirming and legitimizing blockchain transactions. This was especially true in the case of computer-powered cyber money mining [5].

B-Money (1998)

Wei Dei, a computer engineer, unveiled his b-money concept. It was a distributed, decentralized cryptocurrency. It never happened, however, some of the ideas are extremely close to those in Bitcoin. Bitcoin appeared years later. The usage of Proof of Stake was one component. This is an alternate mining method that is based on the developer's current bitcoin holdings rather than sheer processing power [5].

Digital Twins (2002)

The idea and model of the digital twin emerged. It was a virtual representation of something real. In 2002, Michael Grieves made it known to the public. Grieves suggested the notion of the "digital twin" as the foundation for product lifecycle management [5].

Second Life (2003)

An online virtual world is called Second Life. It was created in 2003 at Linden Lab by Philip Rosedale and his group. It served as a strong model for the modern Metaverse worlds being created. Low bandwidth and long "res" times were two of the greatest issues that Second Life users had to deal with. It was therefore not the best experience. However, there are still one million active users of Second Life today. The majority of these users spend a significant amount of time each day in this virtual environment [5].

Roblox (2006)

It was made possible for users to build their games and play those made by other users thanks to this internet platform. It became a significant means of interaction for young people during the 2020 pandemic [5].

Bitcoin (2009)

The bitcoin network started on January 3rd, 2009, when it was first created. Satoshi Nakamoto, its originator, is a mysterious figure. On this date, Bitcoin was created [5].

Blockchain (2009)

Blockchain was created by Satoshi Nakamoto at the same time as Bitcoin. This was supposed to operate as Bitcoin's public transaction ledger. Others have asserted earlier the invention of the blockchain idea [5].

Play-to-Earn Technology (2010)

By early 2010, Japan has become a popular country for Gacha games. It is based on the idea of a capsule toy vending machine, with MapleStory being the first system that is currently known to exist. Players may engage in a random draw from a selection of things by earning cash that they could then spend to do so. This was based on pre-defined rarities, frequently to collect all of one group of objects to get a significant in-game prize [5].

Ready Player One (2011)

Many young individuals were first exposed to virtual reality through Ernest Cline's book. The Steven Spielberg adaption in 2018 increased curiosity and made the concept even more compelling [5].

NFTs (2012)

A non-fungible token (NFT) is one. Instead of fungible tokens, which may be used interchangeably, it represents a singular object. A non-fungible thing is one like cryptocurrencies like Bitcoin. Since December 2012, NFTs have been a notion. It is now official that "Colored Coins" have been created. In this, the extra information is added to a bitcoin, making it unique rather than fungible. This was an intriguing initiative that a young Vitalik Buterin was in charge of. He had been working on enhancing the Bitcoin blockchain. [5].

Vitalik Buterin (2014)

Confinity, owned by Peter Thiel, and X.com, owned by Elon Musk, combined to develop PayPal in 1999. PayPal was acquired by eBay for $1.5 billion three years later. Musk and Thiel became extremely wealthy as a result. The Thiel Fellowship was founded in 2010, according to Peter Thiel. For students under the age of 22, he gave $100,000 subsidies so they may drop out of school and start working elsewhere. Vitalik Buterin, the co-founder of Ethereum, was 20 years old then. He was one of the beneficiaries of this prize in 2014 [5].

Ethereum (2015)

The Ethereum Network was introduced by Gavin Wood and Vitalik Buterin in July 2015. This network and the Ethereum blockchain were both released at the same time [5].

Decentraland (2015)

This virtual reality platform's initial version was released in 2015. It used a proof-of-work method to distribute "land." The 2021 NFT boom has caused some of the game's real estate plots to sell for over $100,000 [5].

Smart Contracts (2015)

Nick Szabo developed the initial idea for smart contracts in the early 1990s. He coined the expression to describe a group of contracts that have been digitally signed. This includes the procedures established by the parties to carry out their duties. Since the debut of the Ethereum blockchain in 2015, the phrase "smart contract" has been used to more clearly characterize the idea of general-purpose computing that takes place on a blockchain or distributed ledger [5].

Pokémon GO (2016)

The first video game to superimpose a virtual environment over the actual one was Pokémon Go. To find, catch, train, and battle virtual monsters known as Pokémon, it makes use of mobile devices with GPS. These simulate being in the player's actual location [5].

The DAO: Decentralized Autonomous Organizations (2016)

In May 2016, The DAO was established through a crowdfunded token sale. At the time, it had established the record for the biggest crowdfunding campaign in history. It was supposed to be a venture capital fund. It was to be built on the Ethereum blockchain. As a result, it would function as a decentralized funding mechanism. Users exploited a vulnerability in The DAO code in June 2016. They were able to siphon off one-third of DAO's cash into a subsidiary account as a result of this. As a result, The DAO as a firm died. However, the notion of decentralized autonomous organizations (DAOs) persists. It has, in fact, significantly improved as a result of the lessons learned from The DAO experience. In the future, each DAO will be an integral component of future metaverse corporations. Participants in the association would govern these enterprises collaboratively. This will conform with the blockchain's laws and financial transactions [5].

Fortnite (2017)

When it first came out, this multiplayer video game was a great hit. It exposed many individuals to the appearance and feel of the metaverse and cryptocurrencies [5].

Dai Stablecoin (2018)

The Dai Stablecoin was created to bring stability to the turbulent crypto ecosystem. Some cryptocurrencies are not tied to any fiat currency and are solely tied to other cryptocurrencies. The centralized Dai Stablecoin, on the other hand, was linked to the US dollar. As a result, it is a significantly less volatile and more dependable coin for decentralized finance (DeFi). Blockchain-based financial services are already available on a variety of platforms. This makes bitcoin borrowing, lending, and investment possible [5].

Decentralized Exchanges (DEX)- (2018)

Bancor, a cyber money exchange, suffered a significant public relations blow after losing $13.5 million to hackers. Their legal/regulatory underpinning is still a little hazy.

However, DEXes continue to be used by people to sell and exchange their cyber currency assets in person. They do it via smart contracts rather than a centralized exchange [5].

Axie Infinity (2018)

Axie Infinity is a popular NFT virtual reality game. It is based on a mythological animal husbandry world. It was released in 2018. It had the largest aggregate value of NFTs of any play-to-earn game platform by mid-2021 [5].

COVID (2020)

People were quarantined all across the world when COVID suddenly appeared in the year 2020. They had limited alternatives for where to spend their time and effort. The metaverse swiftly became the preferred location for an increasing number of young people as a result. It drew gamers and anyone looking to make money online. The metaverse has adopted an anti-establishment tone in response to our divided society. People are being driven to the metaverse's subterranean worlds and economies as a result. This is laying the groundwork for the Metaverse to flourish [5].

Decentralized Apps (Dapps) – (2020)

The drive to eliminate the middleman is still active. This is due to the ongoing emergence of transparent, open-source programs. They support acronymized usage like gaming, DEXes, DeFi, and others. Dapps are frequently referred to be a new trend [5].

First Concert in the Metaverse (2020)

Just under 30 million people watched Travis Scott and Marshmello perform in the online game Fortnite in April 2020 [5].

Solana (2020)

The Solana blockchain dapp was unveiled in April as well. An SOL is a coin used by this dapp. It is mined using an alternative proof of stake (POS) mechanism, unlike Ethereum. Furthermore, Solana addressed and simplified aspects relating to block ownership. "Proof of history" is a novel consensus tool that it uses. This updates its blockchain with timestamps [5].

Alien Worlds (2020)

This incredibly popular dapp was developed with an interplanetary multi-metaverse scenario in mind. To mine tokens and do out other functions, it included NFT characters interacting in a decentralized autonomous organization. More than 2.5 million people have used Alien Worlds by 2021. But its importance extends beyond that. The game is designed to educate players on important lessons about the fundamentals of cryptocurrencies and crypto-mining [5].

Chapter 7
Good Points About Metaverse

The metaverse may grow up being the next major advancement in computer technology for creating and using digital systems [8]. The systems will have digital representations of real-world objects, places, identities, and actions. This chapter discusses the good points about the metaverse.

Collaboration and Linking

Connecting and collaborating with real-world individuals in the virtual world is the main purpose of a metaverse. In the virtual world, people may communicate, work together, and socialize. They can also carry out transactions that apply to the actual world. Using their avatars in the virtual world, real individuals may socialize, party, have meetings, attend virtual conferences, or watch shows [1].

Avatars

As was already noted, 3D avatars serve as users' representations in the metaverse. The behavior of these avatars is those of real individuals. Future XR technology will support touch, smell, and sensation. It will combine mixed reality, virtual reality, and augmented reality (MR). Users of the metaverse use one or more of these XR gadgets to enter the metaverses. These tools produce a simulated environment. They record the player's voice in addition to location information [1].

Virtual Representation of the Real World

The primary idea of the metaverse is to simulate real-world economics. It enables interaction with them in the virtual world followed by a return to the physical one. In a virtual environment, people from the actual world receive training. They pick up knowledge and use it in the actual world. In games where players earn digital currencies and subsequently pay them out in real money, digital assets and NFTs are utilized [1].

High-Performance Computing

High-performance computing is necessary for the creation and operation of metaverses to support all of its components. Most metaverse companies are focusing on building out their high-performance computing infrastructure. Faster processing, storage, and high-speed internet are highlighted [1].

Persistence

This implies that users can enter the virtual world anytime they choose. It may be changed by the user by including additional virtual structures or other items. The following time they visit, these adjustments will still be in effect. Today, user-generated content is a staple of social media. The metaverse will similarly rely on user-generated material, digital works, and personal narratives [1].

Effective remote working

Metaverse can overcome all of the current issues associated with remote work. It provides managers with a virtual environment in which they may interact with employees as avatars. They can talk with them, read their body language, and connect with them in person. They may also maintain track of the team within a virtual workplace. The employer can settle workplace difficulties such as time theft and goldbrick [1].

Healthcare tools

A metaverse is a game-changing tool for healthcare experts and medical staff who could not previously visit patients owing to geographic restrictions. In the Metaverse's virtual reality, they may engage with the patient and obtain a comprehensive picture of their health state [1].

Monetization of benefits

Some developers want to create their business-specific initiatives using the ecosystem. while others hunt for means of making money. Fortunately, the Metaverse can satisfy the requirements of both groups. The Metaverse is open-source, for that reason. On top of that, anyone may build a worthwhile project. People may create and trade NFTs to become regular users of the ecosystem and make money [1].

Chapter 8
Downside in Metaverse

An entirely new age of social and technical encounters is predicted by the metaverse. The interoperability and immersion of these experiences are unmatched. The metaverse has its fair share of drawbacks in terms of privacy and security concerns, just like any other new technology [7]. Platforms for the metaverse are powered by technology, which has hazards of their own.

Interoperability and immersive experiences have drawbacks. A virtual office area may be available to users in the Metaverse. They could also have additional attachments, such as a virtual laptop. This would be identical to an office environment. In these contexts, security and privacy concerns will be of utmost importance. Possible threats include breaches, spying, imposters, and intrusions [1]. Various downsides of the metaverse are discussed further in detail.

Reduced Perception of Physical Space

Both societies and people exist. Humans require family, friends, and meaningful social life. The satisfaction and contentment that real friends and families bring cannot be matched by virtual ones. Time and space in the actual world and the virtual world are not the same. This may alter how we think about space and time. The unknown is the precise adverse effects. But the more virtual worlds we inhabit, the more disconnected from reality we become. The fact is that socializing with actual pals in the real world is not the same as doing so online. [1].

Massive data generation

The metaverse is remaking the physical world into virtual realms. Digital economies are displacing the actual economy. This all demands a substantial amount of 2D and 3D information. The need for data generation, storage, and transport will surely rise as a result. The volume of data we create every day is already generating problems. Because new hardware is being produced daily, this will remain an issue in the future [1].

Cyber-attacks

Millions of cyberattacks happen every day. As a result, maintaining data security in the metaverse will be difficult. The AR and VR technologies that drive the metaverse can lead to several privacy and security issues. This might involve ransomware assaults, identity theft, social engineering attempts, and theft of network credentials. AR and VR systems may have security holes that hackers might exploit. In the metaverse, they can use this to take a user's identity [1].

Virtual identities

It is the same as generating false identities to use avatars and create virtual identities. In the virtual world, you may take on any identity and carry out any task that would be impossible in the physical world. You are capable of participating in several metaverses and having multiple identities. These virtual identities will affect our real selves because of how our bodies and brain function. Some of these behaviors may be with us for a long time [1].

Virtual assets

Virtual asset ownership involves less legal due diligence. Millions of dollars in bitcoin have already been stolen in cyber-attacks. Because everything is linked and online, this problem will only worsen as new metaverses emerge. It is a digitally linked world. As a result, hackers can hack from great distances considerably more easily [1].

Credential Theft

Detecting theft is one of the most challenging metaverse tasks you can undertake right now. In the metaverse, anyone with access to your network credentials might simply assume your identity. Hackers and criminals may utilize wearable technology to steal users' network passwords. One of the biggest worries for merchants using VR and AR-based shopping apps is hacking. Users' financial and personal information kept in their metaverse user accounts might be put at risk due to network credential theft [1].

Perennial threats:

Metaverse creators will have to contend with a multitude of different hazards in addition to hostile assaults. These dangers are frequent on online platforms. It calls into question whether it can shield young consumers from adult content. It will be challenging to prevent our young children from having access to it in the metaverse. Users must also feel secure in the metaverse. Consequently, it will be necessary to address the issue of sexual harassment [1].

Chapter 9
Security Risks in the Metaverse

The metaverse has been challenged by security and privacy issues since its creation. This calls for the creation of a strong cybersecurity infrastructure specifically designed for the metaverse. It will be more difficult to monitor the metaverse and identify assaults on new platforms than on those already in use. With the metaverse, there will be an explosion of gadgets. Construction will soar. Data and apps will multiply. The attack area has just grown by an order of magnitude as a result [1]. Various security risks associated with the metaverse are discussed as follows.

Deepfake

Techniques for creating fraudulent video or audio are now sophisticated enough to be weaponized. They are used to generate targeted material to influence public opinion, stock values, or worse. Deepfakes modify or synthesize visual and audio information using advanced machine learning and artificial intelligence algorithms. It has a significant risk of deceit. This technique might be employed in the metaverse as well. This makes it hard to know whether you're chatting and dealing with a human on the other side of the technology [1].

Immersive attack:

It's a new sort of attack that targets the unique qualities of immersive VR as well as the vulnerabilities that come with them. An Immersive assault might physically or mentally injure or upset the user [1].

Human joystick attack

We perceive ourselves as being within the metaverse since the displays are so near to our eyes. If we have any influence over the environment that someone is in, we effectively have that same influence over that person. Researchers found that by utilizing VR systems, it is feasible to manipulate people who are fully immersed and relocate them to a location in actual space without their awareness [1].

Overlay attack

In such assaults, the hacker superimposes undesirable pictures, videos, or other information onto the player's virtual reality experience. The player won't be able to delete the material. This assault includes fixed, persistent visuals and content in virtual space [1].

Spying in the metaverse

The security expert found that one may listen in on other users within a virtual room in a virtual reality application without that user's knowledge or consent. The phrase "man in the room attack" was created by the researchers to characterize this kind of assault. An assailant may be waiting in the shadows, keeping an eye on and listening to the user [1].

Ransomware

The second most significant threat that VR poses in the metaverse is ransomware. Hackers could put challenging features into VR systems. Users may fall for these tricks and divulge private information. If hostile agents had access to the VR equipment required to reach the metaverse, users' experiences there might be readily jeopardized [1].

Chapter 10
Use Cases of Metaverse

We are aware of the impact that globalization has had on society as a whole. Nearly every area of the earth was supplied with goods created anywhere. Thus, it contributed to raising our level of living. When virtual worlds combine to form one Metaverse, the same type of effect, if not even greater, may be anticipated [4]. Let's examine how the Metaverse might affect several spheres of our lives.

Business and Shopping

There are many difficulties associated with conventional shopping. Because of this, online buying has proliferated. There is no need to be concerned about closure times. When you purchase online, you also don't have to wait in a huge queue of other consumers to get your needs met. Virtual reality will soon be available on standard browsers thanks to WebVR. Checking out the things you love will be easier than ever. Websites do, however, have their restrictions. It is not appealing for your company to include all of its items and variants on its website. People don't also anticipate a website to function like a mall. This is where online shops may help. Virtual stores will replicate the experience of being at a shopping mall. There will never be a temporal or geographical boundary. There will also be personalized digital sales assistants. In any metaverse retail mall, they can give one-on-one service in any language. With the tap of your finger, you will be able to make them appear or disappear. You may check out a toy or piece of jewelry that exists in shop miles and miles away while staying in your room [4].

Even more in-depth information, such as how and where the items were created, will be available for you to examine. Additionally, one may learn what materials were utilized, how long they should endure, etc. Even the performance of the product under various settings and scenarios may be predicted. In other words, if you are purchasing a product in Australia, you can determine how it will function in your city based on its surroundings. The amount of information gathered daily is growing. Therefore, intelligent digital assistants will be able to immediately provide you with items that you could enjoy when you visit a certain store. Virtual intelligent assistants like Siri and Alexa of today will play a significant role [4].

Instead of entering payment information, customers may check out directly from the VR experience. Users may access the virtual residence by inserting their phone into a suitable

VR headset. They may look around to see works by well-known artists from throughout the world. When they are within the virtual setting, they may learn the backstories of each component. After choosing a product, a consumer can add it to their shopping basket. To guard against unintentional purchases, the customer's account will be logged out after removing the headset and closing the application [4].

Education

You can participate in a professional arrangement while still in your classroom. Experts in the field may hold these anywhere in the world. As a result, you could obtain a sense of how the actual world operates. Similar to the previous point, medical students can participate in surgeries performed by experienced doctors anywhere around the globe. They can increase their knowledge in this way. Virtual space centers are accessible to science students. They even get to go on a space mission. It will be simple for teachers and students from different countries to work together. This might raise their level of schooling. Additionally, students can readily present their senior projects for evaluation by professionals throughout the world. They may also relieve any historical occasion thanks to the introduction of virtual reality on the internet. Or they could investigate the atomic and molecular components of any life [4].

Virtual worlds already have a large number of educationally oriented places. These include, among others, Second Life, Kaneva, Cybertown, and Active Worlds. In the online community Second Life, Subquan serves as a learning facility. It takes the place of the conventional math system. It makes use of 3D graphics to aid students in understanding mathematical ideas. The Truths Earth Observation Satellite is another illustration. The collection of data is ten times more accurate than that any other indication. The Virtual University of Edinburgh is a virtual institution for learning and research. It has a focus on bringing everyone in the university together. This can facilitate the use of virtual worlds for study, instruction, and outreach [4].

Advertising

We are aware of the prevalence of adverts nowadays and how bothersome the majority of them are. And we permanently omit a significant amount. However, marketers will soon be able to offer you a more customized ad-viewing experience thanks to precise and in-depth data. Even the best advertisements are understood by the advertisers. Instead of the typical ad system we currently use, every advertisement we encounter will be based on who we are! You may watch commercials while on the run. You may learn about upcoming changes and upgrades for your preferred product [4].

You will be informed right away about a cool store or product while you are in a metaverse. Depending on your metaverse location, you can check it out. The advertisement's message and the plot will also alter. Depending on the modifications you make to a product's design, layout, and other features, this will happen. Additionally, companies will be able to give you virtual tickets to significant events. It is possible to watch the game from the stands [4].

Healthcare

Virtual reality and the metaverse are growing in popularity thanks to human-computer interfaces. It will be easier and more productive than ever to consult with physicians and other health professionals. Anywhere in the metaverse has a hospital unit set up that you can enter. Any doctor in the world is available to you. Your doctor can implant sensors into your body using communication systems like smart dust. Instead of invasive procedures or surgeries, they may quickly identify and cure your problem using straightforward computer software. Doctors will also be able to assign virtual healthcare assistants for you. These virtual assistants will remind you about your medications and exercise. For every activity, you will get live and instant feedback on how they affect your health. When it comes to healthcare, time and awareness is the key factor. Hence, with technology, we will be able to spot any issue way before it brings any threat to us [4].

Office and Workplace

In a metaverse, one may go to a company's virtual corporate headquarters. They can monitor their hiring practices. You may visit offices all around the world just from the comfort of your own home. To be interviewed by the best firms in the world, you do not need to spend any of your valuable time, money, or effort. You may continue working from the comfort of your own home by logging into your metaverse workspace. Your boss can be located somewhere else in the world. However, he may sit next to you and assist you with your job using a 3D avatar that is virtually lifelike [4].

In other words, very soon, the metaverse may serve as the ultimate workplace. There won't be much need for actual things like offices or buildings in the outer world. Just think of the amount of room, money, and labor we could save!

Many virtual businesses already allow workers to work from home. Among them are 10up, Acceleration Partners, AgileBits, and Aids Free World. The future of workplace space may benefit from clever modern initiatives. They may focus on making augmented reality headsets that project holographic data over the actual environment. 3D models may be controlled by the user's hands. Using the flowing virtual displays, they can send emails, explore websites, and write programming. Through the utilization of augmented reality, this contemporary workplace setting replaces conventional keyboards, displays, and even cubicles. Augmented reality may be used flawlessly to enhance the physical environment [4].

Entertainment

You can enter any virtual theatre in the metaverse. Additionally, you may change the screen, the speakers, or even the seating as you choose. As a result, each viewer in a virtual theatre will have a unique experience with the same film. Your immersive experience can be required by the movies themselves. Your interactions with the characters may influence how the tale develops. Similarly, you may use your Metaverse avatar to attend any live events or concerts anywhere around the globe [4].

Revive History

To visit a lovely historical site or museum, one could only need to check in to Metaverse. In a virtual reality museum called Computer Love 2.0, visitors may navigate the exhibits just like they would in the physical world. The University of Sheffield's 3D gallery is furnished with digital replicas of authentic artifacts from three Sheffield Museums. This digital representation is accurate to the analogous physical representation [4].

Tourism and Exploration of Unknown Worlds

Any destination of your choice might be experienced realistically in the metaverse. This may essentially be the future. In the real world, we would all dearly want to travel with our families. However, others would concur that traveling in the actual world might occasionally be risky. It is pricey, to start. A trip to an exotic area will cost you a lot of money. The quantity of legal procedures you must go through to visit a location outside your country is another factor. You could just find the answer in the metaverse. You can just go to a web-based travel agent. You may decide where you want to go and have fun traveling [4].

Chapter 11
Future of the Metaverse

The metaverse is anticipated to be the next important paradigm for how humans connect and use digital networks and technology. It establishes a new level for all virtual encounters. It is not a single technology, equipment, or service offered by a single business. It represents the fusion of several distinct technologies [10]. All of these are developing swiftly for widespread usage. Together, such technologies may give users the impression of being in a three-dimensional, immersive world where they can interact with others and their surroundings as if they were in a shared space [6].

A properly evolved metaverse, however, is more than just an online environment. It also possesses at least two more significant qualities. These characteristics increase its potential as a novel platform with several applications. First, the user experience is probably going to combine both the real and digital/virtual worlds. Second, a local economy is anticipated for the metaverse. This covers commerce and digitally native assets. Although the economy and the

Internet are closely related today, the metaverse may have it's economy [6].

Driving Factors for the Future of the Metaverse

The response of users as well as the results of at least four important variables will determine how the metaverse develops [6]. These factors are discussed as follows.

1. Standardization

The degree of standardization and protocol convergence will have a significant impact on the metaverse's future. Additionally, it relies on the degree of platform interoperability [6]. In order words, concerning the standardization, the future of metaverse will unfold with the answers to the following questions.

- Do all platforms have a single, unified economy?

- Will digital items bought in one metaverse be usable in another?

- Are identities cross-platform persistent?

- Do design and coding standards follow one another?

2. *Market Fragmentation*

The fragmentation of the market is another important element. It will be crucial to monitor how many market leaders appear. Understanding their consumer and business use cases is also necessary [6]. When it comes to this factor, the following questions might try to explore the future of the metaverse.

- How much market competition exists, and how does this impact innovation?
- How much M&A and market consolidation can we expect to see?
- Do various platforms cater to various use cases

3. *User Interface*

Now, how the future plays out will also rely on how intuitive and effortlessly integrated the user interface becomes into daily life [6]. The following questions must serve some path to understanding the upcoming version.

- How user-friendly and mobile will the predominant interface be?

- Does the interface allow for smooth transitions between the digital and physical worlds?

4. Governance

The management of the metaverse ecology makes up the fourth element [6]. It is crucial to assess how well and consistently material and behavior are managed.

- Are digital and intellectual property assets securely protected?
- Are platforms subject to strict governmental supervision or do they mostly rely on self-governance?
- How much confidence and security may be placed in conversations and transactions?
- Do tax jurisdictions and legal responsibility issues have an efficient process in place?

Potential Outcomes for the Future

Case 1: *The metaverse is exceptional at the things it is good at, but it never develops into a platform for all purposes [6]. In such a case, the following scenario is possible.*

- Market fragmentation, lack of a strong player, and excessive customer choice

- Although it works effectively for some applications, user interfaces are challenging to incorporate into daily life.

- Gaming, sports, entertainment, and certain retail have strong consumer adoption rates

- Limited team collaboration, virtual meetings, augmented training/learning, and immersive digital twin usage in the enterprise

- Different countries and areas have different regulations.

The bottom line: In this instance, there will be a niche market for particular applications that will support other technologies without displacing them [6].

Case 2: *Instead of a single metaverse, several significant competitors are contending for market share [6]. In such a situation, the following possibilities could take place.*

- Users have to choose a platform to call "home" because there isn't compatibility

- A highly concentrated market results from active mergers and acquisitions and plenty of cash

- Hardware and software technology innovation is accelerated by competition

- Ecosystems fight for user attention through privileged alliances and content

- Platforms implement effective and robust self-governance

The bottom line: Many apps will find a broad market, but it will be divided among the next tech elite [6].

Case 3: Our primary interface, via which we carry out the majority of our everyday activities, shifts to an open, interoperable metaverse [6]. The following possibilities could be seen.

- The user interface provides a largely seamless merging of the actual and virtual worlds
- Identity in the metaverse is viewed as being equal to identity in the real world
- Numerous creators, many different providers, and an open, interoperable system
- Widespread acceptance for both consumer and business use cases
- Regulations governing digital ownership, privacy, and security that are stringent and enforcement

The bottom line: The current internet will fully transition into the immersive environment that most companies and consumers use [6].

What options do executives have today?

Although the metaverse's future is still uncertain, corporate leaders can already take several steps [6]. The following things should be considered.

- ***Never undervalue the potential:*** Make a plan for the metaverse. However, it must be adaptable enough to adjust to emerging technologies and market tastes. For both consumer-facing and internal processes, use a test-and-learn strategy [6].

- ***Think long-term:*** Businesses should examine their investments over the long term. Along with Return on Investment, they should take into account KPIs (Key Performance Indicators) related to customer and staff engagement (ROI). Additionally, they must take expenditures into account in the context of larger digital transformation goals [6].

- ***Pay attention to user motivations and demand:*** Organizations should concentrate on developing compelling content and experiences. This has to do with unique collaborations, tools for user-generated content, and comprehensive data and insight gathering. This is necessary to gain market share and maintain competitiveness [6].

- ***Become dedicated to a moral metaverse:*** In the metaverse, organizations will have to deal with a variety of hazards and complexity. They must make sure they are actively creating a responsible metaverse and successfully upholding both employee and customer trust [6].

Summary

The metaverse is a technology that has a lot of promise and is highly inventive and fascinating. It has the power to alter how we engage with the online environment. The internet as we know it could transform. Before the metaverse can be completely realized, however, there are still several issues that must be resolved. More user-friendly interfaces need to be made by developers. A better method of generating revenue from virtual worlds is required.

In conclusion, the metaverse is always evolving and growing in popularity. The interest of businesses and consumers in technology is growing constantly. Right now, it looks like the metaverse has a bright future. It will be interesting to see how this virtual world changes over time and how it affects our daily life.

I hope this book provided a clear overview of the Metaverse world. So, comfort yourself with these ideas and attempt to learn more about them as you go.

Good luck.

Be loving & be smiling.

Take care.

- **Vicky V. Choudhary**

References

[1]. Nath, Keshab (2022): Evolution of the Internet from Web 1.0 to Metaverse: The Good, The Bad and The Ugly. TechRxiv. Preprint.

https://doi.org/10.36227/techrxiv.19743676.v1

[2]. Bapodara, Sagar. (2022, January 22). What is Extended Reality? Geeks for Geeks.

https://www.geeksforgeeks.org/what-is-extended-reality/

[3]. Weston, Georgia. (2022, March 21). Know The Key Features of Metaverse. 101 Blockchains.

https://101blockchains.com/metaverse-features/#:~:text=The%20metaverse%20is%20an%20open,metaverse%20alongside%20performing%20other%20transactions.

[4]. Shrusti. (n.d.). The Power and Scope of Metaverse. Srushti Creative.

https://srushticreative.com/wp-
content/uploads/2019/03/THE-POWER-AND-SCOPE-OF-
METAVERSE.pdf

[5]. Frey, Thomas. (2021, September 16). The History of the
Metaverse. Futurist Speaker.
https://futuristspeaker.com/future-trends/the-history-of-the-
metaverse/

[6]. Deloitte. (n.d.). A whole new world? The metaverse and what
it could mean for you.
https://www2.deloitte.com/us/en/pages/technology/
articles/what-does-the-metaverse-mean.html

[7]. Ning, Huansheng & Wang, Hang & Lin, Yujia & Wang,
Wenxi & Dhelim, Sahraoui & Farha, Fadi & Ding, Jianguo
& Daneshmand, Mahmoud. (2021). A Survey on
Metaverse: the State-of-the-art, Technologies,
Applications, and Challenges.
https://www.researchgate.net/publication/356375388_A_Su

rvey_on_Metaverse_the_State-of-the-art_Technologies_Applications_and_Challenges

[8]. J.P. Morgan. (2022, January 18). Opportunities in the metaverse.

https://www.jpmorgan.com/content/dam/jpm/treasury-services/documents/opportunities-in-the-metaverse.pdf

[9]. Lee, Lik-Hang & Braud, Tristan & Zhou, Pengyuan & Wang, Lin & Xu, Dianlei & Lin, Zijun & Kumar, Abhishek & Bermejo, Carlos & Hui, Pan. (2021). All One Needs to Know about Metaverse: A Complete Survey on Technological Singularity, Virtual Ecosystem, and Research Agenda. 10.13140/RG.2.2.11200.05124/8.

https://www.researchgate.net/publication/355172308_All_One_Needs_to_Know_about_Metaverse_A_Complete_Survey_on_Technological_Singularity_Virtual_Ecosystem_and_Research_Agenda

[10]. S. -M. Park and Y. -G. Kim, "A Metaverse: Taxonomy, Components, Applications, and Open Challenges," in IEEE Access, vol. 10, pp. 4209-4251, 2022, DOI: 10.1109/ACCESS.2021.3140175.

https://ieeexplore.ieee.org/document/9667507